STEP·BY·STEP
MOROCCAN
Cooking

KÖNEMANN

MOROCCAN BASICS

B'stilla: Ancient in origin, the B'stilla is the great party piece of every Moroccan banquet. The traditional version is a pie made of incredibly thin, delicate and highly decorated pastry enclosing a mediaeval mix of pounded pigeon, lemon and honey-flavored eggs, chopped almonds and raisins. Modern variations allow the use of filo pastry and shredded chicken.

Cinnamon: The bark of the cinnamon tree contains an essential oil which is released after grinding. Used in moderation, the fragrant odor and sweet spicy flavor of ground cinnamon add a delicious taste to fish and fish sauces. Combined with ground pepper, ginger, cloves and mace, cinnamon makes an excellent dry marinade to rub on game before cooking.

Coriander: Coriander seed is often used in Morocco to make dry marinades for meats. Fresh coriander — cilantro — is used in almost all Moroccan cooking but particularly in salads and salad dressings. Some people are immediately addicted to the sweet yet tart flavor. For others it is an acquired taste. Cilantro is readily available. It can be kept successfully in a refrigerator for a week so long as it is wrapped in a damp kitchen towel and put in a zipped plastic food storage bag.

Couscous: Although traditionally served at the end of the meal, couscous is a substantial meal in itself. It consists of fluffy grains of semolina steamed over a rich soup of meat and vegetables. Couscous is readily available from supermarkets.

Couscousier: Couscous is traditionally cooked in a couscousier, a metal pan topped with a steamer and cover. The meat and vegetables cook in the bottom while the semolina cooks in the top.

Harissa: Harissa is a fiery condiment which is widely used in Morocco and other North African countries. The basic ingredients are hot red chilies, cayenne, olive oil and garlic. It should be thick with the consistency of a light mayonnaise. It is an excellent

accompaniment for saffron-flavored soups and stews. See page 8 for this recipe.

Chickpeas & Lentils: For centuries chickpeas and lentils provided calories and protein for the Moroccan diet when meat was either too difficult or too expensive to procure. Delicious and nutritious, both are available from supermarkets.

Ginger: This extremely pungent spice should be creamy white in color when ground. When using fresh, peel and grate or chop finely. It will keep for months stored in the freezer.

Orange Flower Water: Orange flower water is made from neroli, an essential oil extracted from the flowers or blossom of sweet orange trees.

Widely used as a perfume, its subtle fragrance is also used to flavor pastry, pancakes, custards, confectionery, cordials and fresh salads. It is available from imported food stores, some pharmacies and Middle Eastern food stores.

Parsley: Fresh flat-leaved parsley is also known as Italian parsley. Flat-leaved parsley is used extensively in Moroccan cooking.

Pepper: Pepper is the most widely used spice in Morocco. Freshly ground black pepper lends flavor and excitement to most foods.

Preserved Lemon: See page 4 for recipe.

Saffron: Saffron is a spice made from the dried stigmas of a special kind of crocus. Expensive, only small amounts of it are used, sometimes it is blended with a little ground turmeric, salt and ground sweet paprika to make it go further. Take care when buying. There is no such thing as cheap saffron. To be sure, buy in strands and grind it yourself. Stored in an airtight container in the freezer, it will keep for years.

Tagines: Tagines are long simmered, highly flavored stews of chicken, turkey, or lamb enriched with spices. Many varieties of tagine are served at a banquet.

Moroccan Preserved Lemons

16 thin-skinned lemons
water
coarse salt
lemon juice

1 Wash lemons well. Place in large glass, stainless steel or plastic container. Cover with cold water and allow to soak for 3—5 days, changing water daily.
2 Drain lemons. Insert the point of a sharp knife into peel 1/4 inch from the bud end of each lemon and make four incisions lengthwise to within 1/4 inch of the other end. Then cut through incisions so that lemons are cut completely through both sides, but are still held together at both ends.
3 Insert 1/4 teaspoon coarse salt into center of each lemon, and arrange lemons in sterilized preserving jars and sprinkle with 1 tablespoon coarse salt. Add strained juice of 1 lemon to each jar and pour in enough

Preparation time:
1 hour, spread over 3 days
Preserving time:
3 weeks
Makes 16

boiling water to cover lemons.
4 Store in a dry place and leave for 3 weeks.
5 To use: Rinse well under cold running water. Cut away pulp from each quarter and use peel only.
Note: Preserving jars must be thoroughly clean and sterile before use. After washing and rinsing well, immerse the jars in water in a large pan and boil for 10 minutes to sterilize.

HINT
The peel is used to flavor many Moroccan dishes, and is delicious julienned in salads. Think ahead. Preserve when lemons are on sale.

Wash lemons well. Place in large container and cover with cold water.

Make four incisions lengthwise leaving 1/4 inch at either end uncut.

Spoon *1/4* teaspoon of coarse salt into the center of each lemon.

Pack lemons into jars, add salt, lemon juice and top with boiling water to cover.

Cook veal, onions and pepper in olive oil in a large pan until golden brown.

Add drained lentils and cook for 1 hour, or until veal and lentils are tender.

SOUPS & APPETIZERS

A Moroccan feast often begins with a generous spread of tempting dips and appetizers so that each guest can enjoy a little of everything.

Lentil Soup

Simple and hearty.

Preparation time:
30 minutes:
Cooking time:
$1^1/2 - 2$ hours
Serves 6

$3^1/2$ oz red lentils	6 cups water
2–3 shanks of veal, cut across bone into $1^1/4$ inch pieces	2 large potatoes, finely chopped
2 medium red onions, finely chopped	2 large carrots, finely chopped
ground pepper	1 bunch cilantro, chopped
$1/4$ cup olive oil	lemon juice

1 Cover red lentils with boiling water, leave to stand for 15 minutes.

2 Cook veal, onions and pepper in olive oil in a large heavy-based pan, until golden brown.

3 Add 6 cups water and bring gently to the boil. Skim and add drained lentils. Cook for 1 hour, or until the veal and lentils are tender.

4 Add chopped potatoes and carrots and simmer until vegetables are tender, adding more water if necessary.

5 Remove veal from pan. Remove meat from bones and chop into small cubes. Process soup mixture until smooth.

6 Just before serving the Lentil Soup stir in chopped cilantro, chopped veal and add a squeeze of lemon juice. Adjust seasoning if necessary. Serve with crusty bread.

Add chopped potatoes and carrots and simmer uncovered until tender.

Stir in chopped cilantro, veal and a squeeze of lemon juice before serving.

7

Pumpkin Soup with Harissa

Preparation time:
  10 minutes
Cooking time:
  20 minutes
Serves 6

---

5 lb pumpkin
3 cups chicken stock
3 cups milk
sugar
ground pepper

HARISSA
3¹/4 oz dried red
  chilies
6 cloves garlic, peeled
¹/3 cup salt
¹/2 cup ground
  coriander
¹/3 cup ground cumin
²/3 cup olive oil

---

1 Remove skin, seeds and fiber from pumpkin and cut into pieces. Simmer uncovered in a large pan with stock and milk for 15—20 minutes until tender.

2 Process pumpkin mixture until smooth. Season with a little sugar and pepper.

3 To make Harissa: Wearing rubber or cotton gloves remove stems of chilies. Split chilies in half, remove seeds and soften in boiling water for 10 minutes.

4 Process garlic, salt, ground coriander and cumin, and drained red chilies to a paste, slowly adding olive oil until well combined.

5 Add sufficient Harissa to soup to taste, or serve separately in a bowl.
Note: Store any leftover dried chilies in a jar away from light and heat.

HINT
Add a little cream to the soup for extra richness. Freshly grated nutmeg is also good with pumpkin soup. Harissa is traditionally ground using a mortar and pestle. A great fiery condiment to use with couscous.
To give Harissa extra flavor, dry-fry coriander and cumin seeds just before grinding.
Harissa can be found in well-stocked supermarkets with gourmet or import sections.

Remove pumpkin skin, seeds and fiber before cutting into even-sized pieces.

Add milk and stock and simmer uncovered for 20 minutes until tender.

Wearing rubber or cotton gloves, split chilies and remove stems and seeds.

Stir through Harissa to taste before serving, or serve separately in a bowl.

Eggplant Purée

A popular starter.

Preparation time:
40 minutes
Cooking time:
20 minutes
Serves 4

---

2 lb eggplants, peeled and cut into 3/4 inch cubes
1/3 cup olive oil
2 cloves garlic, crushed
ground pepper

1 teaspoon ground sweet paprika
3 pita breads
1 egg white, lightly beaten
2 tablespoons cumin seeds

---

1 Preheat the oven to 350°F.
2 Steam eggplant cubes in a colander or Chinese bamboo steamer over boiling water for 30 minutes.
3 Heat oil in a large pan until moderately hot.
4 Add eggplant, garlic, pepper and paprika. Reduce the heat a little.
5 Stir constantly for about 10 minutes or until eggplant is very soft. Serve hot with toasted pita bread.
6 To prepare Pita Bread: Split each into two rounds. Brush with egg white, sprinkle with cumin seeds. Bake for 20 minutes, or until crisp. Break pita bread into pieces before serving.
Note: The seed of the cumin plant is often used in Moroccan cooking. Its aromatic scent and pungent flavor is similar to the caraway seed but much stronger. A delicious flavor for steamed or barbecued lamb, cumin can be used whole or ground.

HINT
Steaming the eggplant before frying reduces the amount of oil needed for frying — 1/4 cup oil may be all that is required. It is necessary to salt tough skinned eggplant to remove bitter juices; small tender eggplant will not require salting.

Steam eggplant cubes in a steamer over boiling water for 30 minutes.

Add eggplant, garlic, pepper and paprika to preheated pan.

Stir constantly for about 10 minutes or until eggplant becomes soft.

Brush pita bread with egg white, sprinkle with cumin seeds and bake.

11

Moroccan Cigars

Perfect party food.

Preparation time:
40 minutes
Cooking time:
25—30 minutes
Serves 20

---

1 medium onion,
  finely chopped
1/3 cup olive oil
15 oz lean ground
  beef or lamb
2 teaspoons ground
  cinnamon
1/2 teaspoon ground
  allspice

1/4 teaspoon ground
  ginger
ground pepper
1/2 cup chopped fresh
  parsley
5 eggs
1 lb filo pastry
6 oz butter, melted

---

1 Preheat oven to 300°F. To make Filling: Cook onion in the olive oil until soft. Add beef or lamb, crushing it with a fork. Add seasonings and spices. Cook 10—15 minutes, stirring with a wooden spoon, until meat is well cooked and lump-free. Add parsley.

2 Lightly beat the eggs in a bowl and pour over the meat. Cook for 1—2 minutes, stirring, until egg mixture sets to creamy consistency.

3 Add more spices and seasonings, if desired. Allow the filling to cool.

4 Cut each sheet of filo pastry into three equal-sized rectangles. Place one on top of the other and cover with a damp dish towel.

5 Brush one of the rectangles lightly with melted butter.

6 Place a teaspoon of filling along one of the short edges. Tuck the edge and ends of pastry around the filling, and roll into a cigar shape. Repeat with other rectangles.

7 Place cigars side by side on a greased baking sheet. Brush with melted butter and bake for 25—30 minutes until the cigars are golden. Serve hot.

Stir onion, ground beef and spices until well cooked and lump-free. Add parsley.

Pour lightly beaten eggs over the meat mixture and stir until creamy.

Cut each sheet of filo pastry into three equal sections. Stack onto damp towel.

Tuck edges of pastry around filling and roll over and over to make cigars.

Moroccan-style Brains

Eat hot or cold.

Preparation time:
30 minutes +
1 hour soaking
Cooking time:
15 minutes
Serves 4

---

4 sets of lamb brains
white vinegar
3 cloves garlic, crushed
¹/4 cup olive oil
1 x 14 oz tin peeled
* tomatoes, drained*
1 small bunch flat-
* leaved parsley,*
* finely chopped*
1 small bunch
* cilantro, finely*
* chopped*

1 teaspoon ground
* sweet paprika*
pinch of cayenne
* pepper*
1 teaspoon ground
* cumin*
1 tablespoon lemon
* juice*
rind of 1 preserved
* lemon (see page 4),*
* cut into wide strips*

---

1 Soak the lamb brains in water with 2 teaspoons of vinegar for 1 hour.
2 Remove thin membranes around brains, using a wooden skewer, and wash under cold running water. Cut into largish pieces, removing lobes.
3 Cook garlic in oil in large heavy-based pan until golden. Add tomatoes, parsley, cilantro, paprika, cayenne pepper, cumin, lemon juice and rind. Simmer for 5 minutes.
4 Add brains and cook gently for 10 minutes, turning frequently. Serve immediately.

HINT

Cilantro is often used in Moroccan cooking, particularly in salads and salad dressings. It is readily available; often it is next to the flat-leaved parsley, which looks similar. To avoid confusion, check the label, or gently rub a leaf and smell your finger—the cilantro aroma will be unmistakable.

Carefully remove thin membrane around brains using a wooden skewer.

Wash under cold running water. Cut brains into large pieces, removing lobes.

Add tomatoes, spices, parsley, lemon juice and rind to garlic and oil.

Add brains to mixture and cook gently for 10 minutes, turning frequently.

Cook onions and garlic in oil and butter for 30 minutes on low heat until soft.

Stir in cinnamon, paprika, cumin and coriander and cook for a few minutes.

VEGETABLES, SALADS & BREAD

These colorful combinations of simple vegetables look every bit as good as they taste. Serve them alone or alongside the main meal.

Warm Lentil and Rice Salad

Preparation time:
15 minutes
Cooking time:
30 minutes
Serves 6

---

1 cup brown lentils
1 cup basmati rice
4 large red onions, finely sliced
4 cloves garlic, crushed
1 cup olive oil
1³/4 oz butter
2 teaspoons ground cinnamon

2 teaspoons ground sweet paprika
2 teaspoons ground cumin
2 teaspoons ground coriander
3 green onions, chopped
ground pepper

---

1 Cook lentils and rice in separate pans of water until grains are just tender; drain.

2 Cook the onions and garlic in oil and butter for 30 minutes, on low heat, until very soft.

3 Stir in cinnamon, paprika, cumin and coriander and cook for a few minutes longer.

4 Combine onion and spice mixture with well-drained rice and lentils. Stir in chopped green onions until combined and add ground pepper, to taste. Serve warm.

HINT
Do not use red lentils, which become mushy very quickly and do not retain their shape. It is not necessary to soak lentils prior to cooking but do rinse them thoroughly.

Combine onion and spice mixture with well-drained rice and lentils.

Stir in chopped green onions with rice and lentils, add pepper to taste.

17

Vegetable Couscous

An exotic dish.

Preparation time:
40 minutes +
overnight soaking
Cooking time:
2 hours
Serves 6

2 cups dried chickpeas *1/3 cup vegetable oil* *1 onion, finely chopped* *1 small stick cinnamon* *2 1/2 oz eggplant, cut into 3/4 inch cubes* *3 medium carrots, cut in 1/4 inch rounds* *3 medium new potatoes, cut into 1/2 inch cubes* *5 oz pumpkin, cut into 1/2 inch cubes* *1/4 teaspoon allspice* *3 teaspoons Harissa, or to taste (see page 8)*	*2 cups boiling water* *3 1/2 oz small green beans, cut in 2 inch diagonal slices* *2 zucchini, unpeeled, cut in 1/2 inch rounds* *1 medium, ripe tomato, cut into eight pieces* *1 tablespoon chopped flat-leaved parsley* *1 tablespoon chopped cilantro* *ground pepper* *COUSCOUS* *1 cup couscous* *3/4 cup boiling water* *2 teaspoons butter*

1 Cover chickpeas with cold water, soak overnight. Drain, wash well and cook in large pan, on low simmer for 1 1/2 hours.
2 Heat oil in a large heavy-based pan and cook onion and cinnamon stick over low heat until onion softens.
3 Add eggplant, carrots and potatoes. Cover and cook on low heat for 10 minutes, stirring occasionally with a wooden spoon.
4 Add pumpkin, allspice and Harissa. Pour boiling water over mixture and add chickpeas, beans and zucchini. Stir in tomato just before serving.
5 Simmer, covered, for a further 15 minutes. Garnish with the fresh parsley and cilantro.
6 To prepare Couscous: Pour boiling water on to 1 cup couscous in a bowl.
7 Stir in butter and allow to stand for about 10 minutes.
8 Steam in a pan with a close-fitting lid on low heat for 5 minutes. Serve with vegetables.
Note: Couscous is the name given to both the cooked dish and the raw grain.

> ### HINT
> It is not necessary to salt eggplant before cooking to remove any bitter juices if eggplant is young and fresh.

Add eggplant, carrots and potatoes to onion and cinnamon stick.

Add pumpkin, allspice and Harissa and pour boiling water over vegetables.

Add chickpeas, beans and zucchini. Stir in tomato, and simmer 15 minutes.

Stir butter into couscous and leave to stand 10 minutes before steaming.

19

Spicy Green Beans

Preparation time:
15 minutes
Cooking time:
25—30 minutes
Serves 4

1¹/2 lb young green beans
¹/4 cup vegetable oil
2 cloves garlic, crushed
1 medium, red onion, finely chopped
6 red, ripe tomatoes, peeled and chopped
1 small red chili, finely chopped
²/3 cup hot water

1 Wash beans, drain and dry on absorbent paper. Remove ends.
2 Heat oil in large frying pan. Add garlic and onion and cook until golden and glossy in appearance. Add tomatoes and chili and cook for 2 minutes more. Add whole green beans and stir-fry over high heat for 3 minutes.
3 Add hot water and simmer 10 minutes, or until beans are just tender. Do not overcook. Serve hot.

HINT
Red onions are also called Spanish onions. They are crisp and sweet and wonderful to use in salads, not just for their taste and texture but for the color and contrast they provide.

Wash beans thoroughly, drain and dry on absorbent paper. Remove ends.

Fry onion and garlic until golden. Add tomatoes and chili. Stir to combine.

Add green beans to tomato and onion mixture and stir-fry over high heat.

Add hot water and simmer 10 minutes, or until just tender. Serve immediately.

Tagine of Mixed Vegetables

Preparation time:
15 minutes
Cooking time:
30 minutes
Serves 4

---

4 large potatoes, peeled and chopped in ³/4 inch cubes
2 medium turnips, peeled and chopped in ³/4 inch cubes
3 medium carrots, peeled and cut in ¹/4 x 1 inch lengths
4 medium zucchini, halved and cut in ⁵/8 inch lengths
3 celery stalks, cut diagonally in ⁵/8 inch slices

1 large onion, chopped in ⁵/8 inch cubes
4 cups water
6 cloves garlic
2 tablespoons olive oil
1 small red chili, chopped
1 teaspoon ground cumin
2 tablespoons finely chopped flat-leaved parsley
1 medium onion, chopped finely

---

1 Prepare potatoes and turnips, carrots, zucchini, celery and onions.

2 In a large heavy-based pan bring water to boil.

3 Add potatoes, turnips, carrots, zucchini, celery, onion and garlic cloves. Cook vegetables until tender, about 15–20 minutes (see Note).

4 Heat oil in small pan and cook chili, cumin, parsley and chopped onion over medium heat for 5 minutes.

5 Add onion mixture to the boiled vegetables and their liquid and cook for about 10 minutes or until liquid has reduced and onion is cooked. Serve immediately.

Note: As zucchini cooks more quickly than other vegetables, remove from liquid with a slotted spoon after about 8 minutes. Add to pan with other vegetables.

Prepare and chop potatoes, turnips, carrots, zucchini, celery and onion.

Bring water to boil and add vegetables and garlic cloves. Cook until tender.

Cook chili, cumin, parsley and chopped onion over medium heat for 5 minutes.

Add onion mixture to boiled vegetables and their liquid and cook for 10 minutes.

Grated Carrot Salad

Preparation time:
15 minutes
Cooking time:
Nil
Serves 6

---

10 large carrots
2 small cucumbers
3¹/2 oz raisins
1 tablespoon lemon
juice
¹/2 teaspoon ground
ginger

1 teaspoon ground
cinnamon
1 tablespoon honey
¹/3 — ¹/2 cup olive oil
ground pepper
¹/2 cup flaked
almonds

---

1 Peel and coarsely grate carrots. Place carrots and cucumber in a bowl, add raisins and mix through.

2 Combine lemon juice, ginger, cinnamon, honey, olive oil and pepper in a small bowl or screwtop jar. Whisk or shake well to combine.

3 Place flaked almonds in a small pan, stir over low heat until lightly golden.

4 Pour dressing over salad, garnish with almonds and serve.

HINT
To improve the raisins, soak them in water for 10 minutes until plump.

Peel and coarsely grate carrots.
Combine with cucumber and raisins.

Place flaked almonds in a small pan and stir over low heat until golden.

Pour prepared dressing over salad and stir through until well combined.

Garnish with almonds and serve immediately.

Cucumber Salad with Mint

Preparation time:
15 minutes
Cooking time:
Nil
Serves 6

---

5 small cucumbers	*1/3 cup vegetable oil*
1/4 cup finely chopped fresh mint	*1 teaspoon orange flower water*
1 tablespoon lemon juice	*ground pepper*
	rind of an orange

---

1 Finely peel cucumber and slice thinly. Put in a bowl and add mint.
2 Combine lemon juice, oil, orange flower water and pepper in a small bowl or screwtop jar. Whisk or shake well to combine.
3 Pour dressing over cucumber slices and mix well.
4 Remove pith from orange rind. Cut rind into thin strips, blanch in boiling water and arrange over cucumber slices to serve.

HINT
Small cucumbers do not need to be presalted. However, if using English cucumber, deseed and presalt them in a colander for half an hour to remove any bitter juices.

Finely peel and slice cucumbers thinly and put in a bowl.

Add finely chopped mint. In a separate bowl, combine dressing ingredients.

Pour dressing over cucumber and mint and stir until well combined.

Remove pith from orange rind and cut into thin strips. Blanch in boiling water.

Green Bell Pepper and Tomato Salad

Preparation time:
  15 minutes
Cooking time:
  10 minutes
Serves 6

---

*3 large green bell
  peppers
3 medium, ripe but
  firm tomatoes,
  peeled and seeded*

*VINAIGRETTE
1 tablespoon vinegar
ground pepper
1/2 teaspoon sugar
1 clove garlic, crushed
1/4 cup olive oil*

---

1 Grill peppers by cutting them in half, seeding and broiling cut-side down until skin blisters and blackens.

2 Cook, peel and cut into 3/4 inch pieces.

3 Cut tomatoes into 3/4 inch pieces.

4 Mix pepper and tomato together.

5 To make Vinaigrette: Combine vinegar, pepper, sugar, garlic and olive oil.

6 Pour over salad and allow to stand for 10 minutes to gather flavor.

Note: Garlic grown in Morocco is tiny, red-skinned and sweeter than garlic grown elsewhere.

Grill seeded peppers cut-side down until they blister. Cool and peel.

Chop prepared peppers and tomatoes into 1/2 inch square pieces.

Mix tomatoes and pepper. Combine vinegar, pepper, sugar, garlic and oil.

Add prepared vinaigrette, stand 10 minutes to gather flavor before serving.

Orange Salad

Fruity and refreshing.

Preparation time:
  15 minutes
Cooking time:
  Nil
Serves 6

6 ripe oranges
8 dates, chopped
¹/4 cup blanched
  almonds, slivered
orange flower water
1 tablespoon fresh
  mint leaves,
  chopped
ground cinnamon

1 Peel oranges, removing all pith, and slice crossways.
2 Place in shallow dish with chopped dates and slivered almonds and flavor to taste with orange flower water.
3 Sprinkle lightly with mint and cinnamon and serve. Orange salad is delicious served with cold duck.
Note: To make Blanched Almonds: Put almonds in a bowl. Pour over boiling water until covered. Stand for 1 minute. Discard water and skins should slip easily away. Sliver with a sharp knife.

HINT
Orange flower water is available at some pharmacies and Middle Eastern food stores.

Wash and peel oranges taking care to remove all pith from the fruit.

Slice oranges crossways into even-sized rounds and place in a shallow dish.

30

Combine chopped dates and slivered almonds with orange slices.

Flavor with orange flower water. Sprinkle with mint leaves and cinnamon.

Khobz
(Whole Wheat
Flat Bread)

Preparation time:
  60 minutes
Cooking time:
  12 minutes
Makes 16

2¹/2 cups whole wheat flour	*1/2 teaspoon ground sweet paprika*
1 teaspoon sugar	*1/3 cup cornmeal*
1 teaspoon salt	*1 tablespoon oil*
1 x ¹/4 oz sachet yeast	*1 egg, lightly beaten*
1¹/4 cups tepid water	*2 tablespoons sesame seeds*

1 Preheat oven to 350°F. Combine ¹/2 cup flour, sugar, salt, yeast and water in bowl. Stand, covered, in a warm place until foaming.

2 Sift remaining flour, paprika and cornmeal into bowl, add oil. Stir in yeast mixture. Mix to firm dough. Knead until smooth. Stand, covered, in a warm place 20 minutes.

3 Divide into sixteen, roll into balls, flatten into rounds.

4 Place on greased baking sheet. Brush with egg, sprinkle with sesame seeds. Stand, covered, until puffed. Bake 12 minutes.

Add prepared yeast mixture to oil, flour, cornmeal and paprika.

Mix into a firm dough. Knead until smooth and stand in a warm place.

Divide dough into sixteen even portions. Roll out balls into 4 inch flat rounds.

Brush bread with beaten egg, sprinkle with sesame seeds and bake.

Rub fish with salt, prick several times on each side with a fork and place in a dish.

Stir in tomatoes, tomato sauce and parsley or cilantro to onion mixture.

Spoon the remaining sauce over the fish until it is completely covered.

Sprinkle with the remaining blanched almonds and cover dish tightly with foil.

SEAFOOD

*The Moroccan coastline abounds in seafood. Fish is often marinated
before cooking to develop its full flavor. The results are worth waiting for.*

Whole Baked Fish

Hot and spicy.

Preparation time:
30 minutes +
2 hours standing
Cooking time:
45 minutes
Serves 4—5

---

*1 x 3 lb whole fish,
cleaned*
1/2 teaspoon salt
*2 tablespoons lemon
juice*
*2 onions, sliced top to
base in 1/2 inch slices*
3 cloves garlic, crushed
2 tablespoons olive oil
*1 green bell pepper,
seeded and sliced in
1 1/2 x 1/2 inch slices*
*1 red bell pepper,
seeded and sliced in
1 1/2 x 1/2 inch slices*
*1–2 red chilies, seeded
and thinly sliced*

*1/2 teaspoon ground
turmeric*
*1/2 teaspoon curry
powder*
*5 or 6 small tomatoes,
chopped*
*2 tablespoons tomato
ketchup*
*2 tablespoons cilantro
or parsley, chopped*
*2 3/4 oz blanched
slivered almonds,
finely toasted*
*1 lemon, cut into
wedges*

---

1 Preheat oven to
350°F. Rub fish with
salt and prick several
times on each side
with a fork. Place fish
in a dish and squeeze
lemon juice over it.
Leave for 2 hours.
2 Cook onions and
garlic in the olive oil
until soft. Add the
bell pepper, chilies,
turmeric and curry
powder. Cook gently
for several minutes.
Stir in tomatoes,
tomato ketchup and
chopped cilantro or
parsley.
3 Scatter half the
blanched almonds in
a baking dish. Put in
half the sauce and
then the fish and its
marinade. Spoon
remaining sauce over
the fish. Sprinkle
with remaining
blanched almonds
and cover dish tightly
with foil.
4 Bake in oven for
30 minutes. Remove
foil and bake another
10—20 minutes. Fish
should feel firm to the
touch when ready.
Serve immediately,
garnished with lemon
wedges.

> HINT
> Parsley can be kept in the
> refrigerator. Wrap in wet
> paper towel and put in
> a zipped plastic bag.

Moroccan Fish with Fresh Tomato Sauce

Preparation time:
30 minutes +
3 hours standing
Cooking time:
5 — 10 minutes
Serves 6

1¹/2 lb boneless white fish, skinned
1 medium red onion, peeled and finely chopped
1 clove garlic, crushed
2 tablespoons chopped cilantro
¹/3 cup chopped flat-leaved parsley
¹/2 teaspoon ground sweet paprika
¹/4 teaspoon chili powder
¹/3 cup olive oil
2 tablespoons lemon juice

TOMATO SAUCE
4 large, red, ripe tomatoes, peeled, seeded and chopped
2 small red chilies, cut in half, seeded and finely sliced
4 green onions, including some green, finely sliced
¹/2 bunch cilantro, chopped finely
¹/2 cup extra virgin olive oil
ground pepper
lemon or lime juice (optional)
1 red onion, finely chopped (optional)

---

1 Cut fish across grain into ³/4 x ³/4 inch squares. Combine onion, garlic, cilantro parsley, paprika, chili powder, olive oil and lemon juice and spoon over fish cubes. Mix well and leave to marinate for at least 2 hours or overnight.

2 Place fish on metal skewers and broil, turning frequently until lightly browned on all sides.

3 To make Tomato Sauce: Combine tomatoes, chilies, green onions and cilantro in a bowl, add olive oil and pepper to taste.

4 Add lemon or lime juice and chopped onion if using.

5 Allow the Tomato Sauce to stand for at least an hour in refrigerator before serving with fish.
Note: Fish could be barbecued instead of broiled. This type of tomato sauce, called 'Salsa', makes a very good quick sauce for broiled or fried fish. Allow tomatoes to drain in a strainer for at least 30 minutes to get rid of excess water.

HINT
Extra virgin olive oil is made from the first pressing of olives. No heat or chemicals are used so all the natural flavors are retained.

Spoon onion mixture over fish and mix well. Marinate for 2 hours or overnight.

Carefully thread marinated fish cubes onto metal skewers at regular intervals.

Broil or barbecue fish, turning frequently until lightly browned on all sides.

Combine sauce ingredients and refrigerate at least 1 hour before serving.

Moroccan-style Fish with Dates

Preparation time:
30 minutes
Cooking time:
25 minutes
Serves 2

---

2 medium trout
1 cup chopped dates
1/4 cup cooked rice
1 onion, finely chopped
1/4 cup chopped almonds
2 tablespoons chopped cilantro
1/2 teaspoon ground cinnamon

1 oz butter, melted
1/4 teaspoon ground pepper
1/4 teaspoon ground ginger
1 teaspoon sugar
1/4 teaspoon ground cinnamon

---

1 Preheat oven to 315°F. Clean trout, rinse under cold water. Dry with sheets of absorbent paper.
2 Combine dates, rice, onion, almonds, cilantro and cinnamon in bowl.
3 Spoon seasoning mixture into fish cavities, close opening with metal skewers. Place on baking sheet.
4 Brush fish with melted butter, sprinkle with combined pepper, ginger and sugar. Bake for 20 minutes, or until golden. Sprinkle Moroccan-style Fish with cinnamon, before serving.

HINT

A dark red brown spice with a strong spicy-sweet flavor, cinnamon is actually the bark of a tropical tree. When ground, the bark releases an aromatic essential oil. Used in moderation, the perfume and flavor of ground cinnamon add a delicious taste to fish and fish sauces. Combined with ground pepper, ginger, cloves and mace, it makes an excellent dry marinade to rub on meats before cooking. Store in a sealed container.

Clean and rinse trout. Chop dates, onion, almonds, cilantro and cinnamon.

Mix dates, rice, onion, almonds, cilantro and cinnamon until combined.

Spoon seasoning mixture into fish cavities and close with metal skewers.

Brush fish with melted butter and sprinkle with combined sugar and spices.

Cook chicken in batches until well browned, but not cooked through.

Add remaining oil to pan. Cook onion and bell pepper over a low heat.

POULTRY

Cinnamon, coriander and cumin are just some of the rich variety of flavors and spices used in these fragrant and delicious recipes.

Chicken and Olives

Serve with rice.

Preparation time:
30 minutes +
1 hour standing
Cooking time:
40 minutes
Serves 6

---

12 chicken pieces
1 teaspoon ground cinnamon
1 teaspoon ground ginger
1/2 teaspoon ground turmeric
1 teaspoon ground sweet paprika
1/2 teaspoon ground pepper
1/4 cup olive oil

2 onions, chopped
1 red bell pepper, chopped
1/4 cup cilantro, chopped
1 1/2 cups chicken stock
4 strips preserved lemon rind, grated (see page 4)
2 tablespoons lemon juice
1 cup green olives

---

1 Combine chicken with spices in large bowl. Stand, covered, for 1 hour. Heat 2 tablespoons oil in a large pan. Cook chicken until well browned, but not cooked through. Transfer chicken to larger pan.

2 Add remaining oil to pan. Add onion and bell pepper. Cook over low heat for 5 minutes, stirring. Transfer to large pan with chicken pieces.

3 Add cilantro and stock, lemon rind, juice and olives.

4 Simmer, covered, for 40 minutes, until tender and liquid has reduced.

Add cilantro and stock to chicken and bell pepper mixture, stir to combine.

Add lemon rind, juice and olives and simmer uncovered for 40 minutes.

Steamed Chicken with Parsley Stuffing

Preparation time:
  15 — 20 minutes
Cooking time:
  1¹/2 hours
Serves 6 — 8

2 lb ripe tomatoes, peeled, seeded and chopped
1 large bunch flat-leaved parsley, finely chopped
2 celery stalks, finely chopped
rind of 1 preserved lemon, finely chopped (see page 4)
ground pepper
¹/2 teaspoon chili powder or cayenne pepper
2 x 3 lb fresh chickens
¹/2 oz butter
2 cups water
1 oz butter, melted
ground cumin, to serve
sea salt, to serve

1 Preheat oven to 350°F. Mix the tomatoes with parsley, celery and lemon rind, season with pepper and chili powder.

2 Press stuffing mixture into each chicken, adding half of butter to each.

3 Place chickens in a baking dish with water. Brush with melted butter and cover with foil.

4 Cook for 1¹/4 — 1¹/2 hours, or until tender.

5 Serve at once with little bowls of cumin and sea salt as garnish.

Note: Fresh flat-leaved parsley, also known as Italian, is used extensively in Moroccan cooking and is widely available. Avoid using common or curly parsley. The smell and flavor are not as sweet and pungent.

HINT
During winter months it is better to use canned tomatoes. For 2 lb tomatoes, substitute 2 x 14 oz cans of whole peeled tomatoes, drained. This dish is also good served cold.

Mix tomatoes, parsley, celery and lemon rind. Season with pepper and chili.

Press stuffing mixture into each chicken cavity and add half of butter to each.

Arrange chickens in a baking dish and fill the dish with 2 cups of water.

Brush chickens with melted butter, cover with foil and bake. Serve at once.

Moroccan Chicken

Moist and fragrant.

Preparation time:
30 minutes +
overnight
soaking
Cooking time:
1¹/₄ hours
Serves 6

---

12 chicken pieces
¹/₂ teaspoon ground
sweet paprika
¹/₂ teaspoon ground
cumin
ground pepper
1¹/₂ lb red or brown
onions, sliced
3¹/₂ oz butter
¹/₄ teaspoon ground
saffron or turmeric

4 oz chickpeas,
soaked overnight
3 cups chicken stock
¹/₃ cup finely chopped
flat-leaved parsley
1 tablespoon fresh
lemon thyme (see
Note)
8 oz rice, cooked
lemon juice

---

1 Season chicken with paprika, cumin and pepper.

2 Cook chicken pieces with sliced onions in butter in a deep heavy-based pan until golden.

3 Sprinkle chicken with saffron, add chickpeas and chicken stock to cover. Simmer gently, uncovered, for 1 hour or until chicken is tender.

4 Just before serving add chopped parsley and thyme to chicken.

5 Spoon rice into heated serving dish. Place chicken pieces on top and pour over the sauce. Sprinkle with lemon juice and serve.

Note: Thyme is one of the most popular herbs used in cooking. The lemon variety used in this recipe has a faint lemony smell, as its name suggests.

HINT
Ground sweet paprika, warmly aromatic and rich red in color, is used to add color and flavor to many Moroccan tagines and salad dressings.

Season chicken with paprika, cumin and pepper. Cook with onions until golden.

Sprinkle chicken pieces evenly with ground saffron, and add chickpeas.

Add chicken stock to cover chicken pieces and simmer gently.

Add chopped parsley and thyme to chicken pieces just before serving.

B'stilla (Shredded Chicken Pie)

Preparation time:
45 minutes
Cooking time:
2 hours 15 minutes
Serves 8 entrée size

FILLING
1 x 3 lb chicken
1 large onion, finely chopped
1 large bunch flat-leaved parsley, chopped
1 bunch cilantro, chopped
1/4 teaspoon ground turmeric
1/4 teaspoon ground saffron
2 tablespoons vegetable oil
1 teaspoon ground ginger
1 teaspoon ground cinnamon
1 1/2 cups water

SAUCE AND PASTRY
5 eggs, lightly beaten
1 cup confectioners' sugar
ground cinnamon
ground pepper
1 lb filo pastry
8 oz unsalted butter
1 cup ground almonds
ground cinnamon
1 cup confectioners' sugar, extra

---

1 Preheat oven to 350°F. Place chicken, onion, parsley, cilantro, turmeric, saffron, oil, ginger and cinnamon in a roasting dish with water. Bake for 1 1/2 hours. Remove the chicken from pan and cool. Shred flesh, discard skin and bones.

2 Skim fat from liquid in roasting pan and transfer to medium-sized pan. Bring liquid to a simmer and add beaten eggs, sugar, cinnamon and pepper, to taste. Cook until thick.

3 Preheat oven to 375°F. Grease an 8 inch pie dish.

4 Place a sheet of filo in prepared dish. Brush lightly with melted butter. Place a second sheet on top and brush with butter. Repeat layering and light buttering with seven more sheets, sprinkling some of the combined ground almonds, cinnamon and confectioners' sugar on the last sheet.

5 Spread egg mixture and chicken filling on top, fold over pastry edges and brush again with butter. Butter and layer four more sheets, cut into a round and cover pie. Butter more sheets of filo and form into rose shapes. Place on top of pie and brush with melted butter.

6 Bake for 30—45 minutes until golden brown. Sprinkle with rest of combined almond mixture.

HINT
Ground spices keep their flavor longer if stored in the freezer.

Remove skin and flesh from baked and cooled chicken and discard bones.

Add combined eggs, sugar, cinnamon and pepper to simmering roasting liquid.

Spread chicken filling over layered and lightly buttered filo pastry. Fold in edges.

Form buttered filo into rose shapes and place on pie until surface is covered.

Rub lamb with half the softened butter and season generously with pepper.

Combine onion, garlic and spices, then add olive oil and water and mix well.

MEAT

Whether marinated and slowly roasted or simmered in a spicy broth, this selection of mouth-watering dishes is fit for a feast.

Roast Lamb with Spices

Preparation time:
30 minutes
Cooking time:
1¹/2 — 2 hours
Serves 6

1 x 6 lb leg of lamb	*¹/4 teaspoon ground*
3¹/2 oz unsalted	*cinnamon*
butter, softened	*¹/4 teaspoon ground*
ground pepper	*ginger*
1 large red onion,	*pinch of chili powder*
finely chopped	*¹/4 teaspoon ground*
2 cloves garlic,	*saffron*
crushed	*¹/3 cup olive oil*
¹/2 teaspoon ground	*water*
cumin	

1 Preheat oven to 325°F. Rub lamb with half the softened butter and season generously all over with ground pepper.

2 Make spice mix by combining onion and garlic in a bowl with spices, then add olive oil and water. Mix well with a small whisk or fork.

3 Press half the mixture over buttered lamb. Place remaining mixture in a baking dish big enough to hold the lamb comfortably. Add the rest of the butter to baking dish and place lamb on top. Leave at room temperature for at least 1 hour before baking.

4 Bake for 1¹/2 — 2 hours, basting with pan juices, until lamb is brown and crisp-skinned.

Press half the mixture over the buttered lamb. Place remainder in baking pan.

Bake until brown and crisp-skinned, basting frequently with pan juices.

49

Lamb with Fava Beans and Artichokes

Preparation time:
15 minutes
Cooking time:
1½ hours
Serves 6

---

4 lb lamb shoulder
  chops, trimmed
1½ teaspoons
  ground ginger
1 teaspoon ground
  saffron
2 cloves garlic,
  crushed
2 tablespoons
  vegetable oil
ground pepper

3 cups water
2 lb fresh fava beans,
  shelled
1 x 14 oz can
  artichoke hearts
rind of 1 preserved
  lemon (see page 4)
1 tablespoon lemon
  juice
10 small black or
  green olives

---

1 Place lamb chops in large heavy-based pan, with ginger, saffron, garlic, oil and pepper.

2 Add water, cover and cook gently for 1½ hours or until lamb is tender. If necessary add more water to keep the lamb immersed.

3 Remove lamb from cooking liquid. Skim off any fat.

4 Cook fava beans in boiling water until tender, about 6 minutes. Drain and set aside.

5 Reduce cooking liquid from lamb until sauce is thickened slightly.

6 Return the lamb, beans and reduced cooking liquid to pan. Add artichokes and preserved lemon rind cut into small pieces. Simmer uncovered over very low heat for about 15 minutes, until reheated.

7 Sprinkle with lemon juice and olives, to serve.

> **HINT**
> Artichokes can be replaced with canned, drained, peeled tomatoes.

Place lamb chops and spices in large pan. Cover with water and simmer.

Cook fava beans in boiling water until tender, about 6 minutes, and drain.

Return the lamb to the reduced liquid in the large pan and add the beans.

Add the artichokes and lemon rind to the beans and lamb. Stir to combine.

51

Barbecued Lamb with Chermoula

Marinate overnight.

Preparation time:
25 minutes
+ 3 hours
standing
Cooking time:
45 minutes
Serves 6

---

1 medium onion, grated
2 cloves garlic, crushed
4 tablespoons chopped flat-leaved parsley
4 tablespoons chopped cilantro

1/2 teaspoon ground cumin
1/2 teaspoon ground saffron
1/2 teaspoon Harissa (see page 8)
1/2 cup olive oil
2 tablespoons lemon juice
1 x 1 lb leg of lamb

---

1 To make Chermoula: Mix onion, garlic, flat-leaved parsley, cilantro, cumin, saffron, Harissa, olive oil and lemon juice together in a bowl. When the mixture has combined, leave to stand for 1 hour.

2 Starting at the thicker end of the leg of lamb, cut down and around bone. Scrape away as much meat as possible. Remove bone. Cut down into, but not through, the thickest part of the meat and open out flat.

3 Spread Chermoula mixture into both sides of lamb and marinate for at least 2 hours.

4 Barbecue for about 3/4 hour, turning the lamb frequently. When ready, cut the meat in thick slices across the grain and serve.

Note: If you are short of time, or don't feel confident about doing it, ask your butcher to remove the bone from leg of lamb. Harissa is delicious served with poached eggs or sausages.

Prepare onion, garlic, parsley, cilantro, cumin, saffron, Harissa, oil and lemon.

Mix Chermoula ingredients until well combined and stand for 1 hour.

Remove bone, cut into the thickest part of the meat and open out flat.

Spread Chermoula mixture onto both sides of the lamb and marinate.

Tagine of Lamb with Quinces

Preparation time:
30 minutes
Cooking time:
1 hour
Serves 6

---

2 lb shoulder of lamb, cut in 3/4 inch pieces
2 large onions, chopped in 1/2 inch cubes
ground pepper
1/2 teaspoon ground mildly hot paprika
1 bunch cilantro, finely chopped
1/4 teaspoon ground saffron
1/2 teaspoon ground ginger
1 lb quinces, cored, halved and peeled
2 oz butter
1 cup pitted prunes, pre-soaked

---

1 Place cubed lamb and one of the chopped onions in a large heavy-based pan. Season to taste with pepper and paprika and cover with water.

2 Add cilantro, saffron and ginger. Bring to the boil, reduce heat, cover and simmer for about an hour, or until lamb is tender.

3 Cut the quinces into roughly the same sized pieces as the meat. Cook the quinces and the second onion together in butter in a pan until lightly golden colored.

4 Halfway through cooking time for the lamb, add cooked onion, quinces and prunes. Serve on a warmed serving dish.

Note: Ground paprika is also available in hot and mildly hot strengths. Substitute hot paprika if a spicier flavor is preferred.

HINT
Dates could be used instead of prunes and pears instead of quinces — or in combination with each other.

Season the lamb and onion with paprika and pepper. Cover with water.

Add cilantro, saffron and ginger and mix well. Simmer until tender.

Cook the quinces and onion together in butter until golden colored.

Halfway through the lamb cooking time, add the onions, prunes and quinces.

Moroccan Rice and Meat Balls

Preparation time:
30 minutes
Cooking time:
45 minutes
Serves 8

6½ oz short-grain rice
1 lb finely ground lamb or beef
1 teaspoon ground cinnamon
1 teaspoon ground sweet paprika
1 teaspoon ground coriander
5 oz butter or ghee

2 large onions, finely chopped
¼ teaspoon ground saffron
ground pepper
2 cups water or light stock
¼ cup chopped fresh flat-leaved parsley
2 tablespoons lemon juice

---

1 Using a fork, mix rice with finely ground lamb, add cinnamon, paprika and coriander and shape the mixture into about twenty even-sized small balls.

2 Melt butter or ghee in a heavy-based deep pan.
3 Brown the balls in the butter, a panful at a time, turning frequently.
4 When all balls are browned, add onions, saffron and pepper.
5 Pour in the water or stock, cover and cook over medium heat for about 40 minutes, or until cooked through, stirring occasionally.
6 Add flat-leaved parsley and lemon juice and simmer for a few minutes. Serve Moroccan Rice and Meat Balls with a green vegetable or salad.

HINT

Flat-leaved or Italian parsley has a much better flavor than curly parsley and should be used if available. Ground saffron is available from most supermarkets. Well-stocked supermarkets and specialty stores sell saffron threads.

Using a fork mix rice, finely ground lamb, cinnamon, paprika and coriander.

Carefully shape mixture into about twenty small, even-sized balls.

When all the balls are evenly browned, add onions, saffron and pepper.

Add water or stock to meat balls, cover and cook for about 40 minutes.

Pour combined orange and lemon juices over sliced apples and pears.

Peel and slice bananas diagonally into thin sections and add to fruit bowl.

DESSERTS

The splendid variety of fruits available in Morocco are a refreshing way to end a meal. Desserts and pastries are reserved for special occasions.

Moroccan-Style Fresh Fruit Salad

Preparation time:
20 minutes
Cooking time:
Nil
Serves 6

---

2 apples
2 pears
2/3 cup orange juice
1 tablespoon lemon juice
2 bananas
2 tablespoons orange flower water

confectioners' sugar
8 oz strawberries, hulled and halved lengthways
fresh mint leaves
rind of 1 orange

---

1 Core apples and pears and cut into thin slices.
2 Place in serving bowl and add orange and lemon juices to prevent the apples and pears discoloring.
3 Peel and cut bananas thinly. Add to fruit in bowl and toss gently. Add orange flower water and sprinkle with confectioners' sugar to taste.
4 Add strawberry halves to fruit salad. Sprinkle with fresh mint leaves.
5 Grate orange rind and cook in water or light sugar syrup for 5 minutes, drain. Arrange over fruit salad and serve.
Note: Cutting the strawberries helps to develop the flavor.

HINT
When buying strawberries, look for even-colored, plump berries with fresh, leafy green tops.

Add strawberry halves to fruit salad. Sprinkle with fresh mint leaves to garnish.

Slice orange rind into thin matchsticks and cook in prepared syrup 5 minutes.

Almond Macaroons

Preparation time:
30 minutes
Cooking time:
15—20 minutes
Serves 6

---

*5 oz confectioners'
sugar, sifted
1 egg, beaten
7 oz ground almonds
2 teaspoons finely
grated lemon rind*

*1 teaspoon vanilla
extract
1/4 teaspoon ground
cinnamon
extra confectioners'
sugar, for garnish*

---

1 Preheat oven to 350°F. In a large mixing bowl combine confectioners' sugar and beaten egg. Beat until mixture is white.
2 In another bowl combine ground almonds, lemon rind, vanilla extract and cinnamon and gradually mix into beaten sugar and egg mixture.

3 Knead dough in bowl until pliable, about 5 minutes. Cover with dish towel and leave to mature for 15 minutes.
4 On a lightly floured surface roll out dough to a long thin sausage shape about 1 1/2 inches thick. Cut into twenty-four segments

and roll each segment into an even-sized ball.
5 Lightly oil the palms of your hands and flatten each ball into rounds about 1 1/2 inches in diameter.
6 Place cookies on a buttered cookie sheet, giving them plenty of room to spread while baking, and sprinkle with confectioners' sugar. Bake for 15—20 minutes, or until golden. Cool on wire rack. Store in airtight container.
Note: Serve with Moroccan-Style Fruit Salad (see page 59).

(see page 59)

HINT
Almonds are one of the world's most popular nuts. To keep, store covered tightly in a cool, dark place.

Combine egg and sugar and add to ground almond mixture.

On a floured board, roll mixture into a sausage shape and cut into 24 slices.

Roll each slice into a ball with oiled
hands and flatten into 1^1/$_2$ inch rounds.

Place on prepared sheet and sprinkle with
confectioners' sugar. Bake until golden.

Fried Moroccan Bread with Cinnamon

Preparation time:
15 minutes
Cooking time:
10 minutes
Serves 4—6

½ French bread stick
1—2 eggs
1 cup milk
½ teaspoon vanilla
*   extract*
butter

¼ cup sugar
1 tablespoon ground
*   cinnamon*
½ teaspoon ground
*   nutmeg*

1 Cut French bread stick into ¾ inch thick slices, diagonally.

2 In a bowl, beat eggs until well mixed, add milk and vanilla extract and mix again.

3 Melt butter in frying pan.

4 In a shallow bowl, combine sugar, ground cinnamon and nutmeg.

5 Dip pieces of bread into egg and milk mixture and cook in melted butter until crisp and golden on both sides. Place on absorbent paper and then dip immediately into sugar mixture. Add more butter to frying pan if necessary.

Note: Very good with coffee for an indulgent breakfast.

Cut French bread stick diagonally into ¾ inch thick slices.

In a bowl, beat eggs, milk and vanilla extract until well combined.

Dip pieces of bread into egg and milk mixture and cook in melted butter.

Dip fried bread into combined sugar, cinnamon and nutmeg immediately.

INDEX